ஒளவையார் அருளிய ஆத்திசூடி

Auvaiyaar's Aathisoodi

(A Text of Moral Quotations)

Translated into English

by

Karthik Jayaraman

Vidyuth Publications, Chennai, India

(www.vidyuthpublications.com)

2013 Vidyuth Publications

(www.vidyuthpublications.com)

For Vidyuth, Prahlad and Suhruth

Foreword

This work in Tamil starts with the phrase "Aathisoodi" and hence named as such. It contains 109 compact advisory statements on moral values in which are enshrined the aspects of a universal code of conduct which have stood the test of time.

Simplicity is the hallmark of this poem. It is believed that the poetess Auvaiyaar belonged to the 10th century (C.E). She has also authored several other works like Nalvazhi,

Vaakkundaam and so on. Some scholars are of the opinion that the poetess who rendered this poem is perhaps different from the one having the same name who lived during the last Tamil Sangam period.

It is a great gift to the younger generation as it contains the quintessence of worldly wisdom and good conduct. It is essential that our children learn this when they are young. It will provide them with wise counseling throughout their lives; and shape them into responsible and exemplary citizens of the future, as opined by the Saint Kanchi Mahaperiyavaal.

Mr. Karthik Jayaraman has done a good job in translating these meaningful lines into English. Auvaiyaar has rendered this poem for the benefit of humanity. Therefore, it is only proper that Mr. Karthik Jayaraman has brought it within the scope of understanding of the English-knowing public. It is a commendable service.

Dr.S.Sundaram
Professor of Chemistry (Retired)
Sri Ramakrishna Mission
Vivekananda College, Chennai.

Introduction

Aathisoodi is an ancient moral text (alphabetic acrostic poem) consisting of 109 moral quotations written originally in Tamil language by a respected elderly saint poetess Auvaiyaar. She is believed to have lived in the 10th century in TamilNadu, one of the southern states in India. Aathisoodi literally translates to "wearer (soodi) of a garland made of Orchid (Aathi) flowers". These quotations are tiny capsules filled with infinite moral values that need to be imbibed from childhood. All the quotations start with or contain the 12 vowels, 1 glotaliser (the letter ஃ in Tamil), 18 consonants and 78 combinant letters (of vowels and some consonants) of the Tamil language. By learning, memorizing and understanding the meaning of these quotations from childhood, children will surely gain knowledge of the Tamil letters in addition to the moral values. In this publication, the original quotation in Tamil is provided with the meaning of the quote in English.

Acknowledgments

The idea of embarking on an English translation of Aathisoodi occurred to me while reading the book "The Voice of God"(compiled by Sri Ra. Ganapathy) which is a collection of discourses by Jagadguru Sri Chandrasekharendra Saraswati Swamigal (Kanchi Mahaperiyavaal). Kanchi Mahaperiyavaal had glorified the value of Aathisoodi and stressed the importance of imparting the moral knowledge contained in this text to all the children. Firstly, I offer my humble salutations to Kanchi Mahaperiyavaal.

I would like to extend my sincere thanks to all the personnel behind the online portal www.tamilvu.org for providing free public access to the simple commentaries in Tamil on the ancient text Aathisoodi. The lucid commentaries written by the great Tamil scholar Navalar Thiru Na. Mu. Venkatasamy Nattar served as a significant guidance for me in understanding the meaning of the quotations and attempt an idiomatic translation into English.

ஆத்திசூடி

கடவுள் வாழ்த்து
(Invocation to God)

ஆத்தி சூடி யமர்ந்த தேவனை

ஏத்தி யேத்தித் தொழுவோ மியாமே

Let us always respectfully praise the Lord (Ganesha) who is sitting on the lap of the Lord (Shiva) who is wearing a garland made of Orchid (Aathi) flowers.

Text

1. அறஞ்செய விரும்பு.

Love to do good deeds (actions).

2. ஆறுவது சினம்.

Nature of anger is to quiet down. (or) Quieten your anger.

3. இயல்வது கரவேல்.

Offer everything within your means to people in need.

4. ஈவது விலக்கேல்.

Do not prevent an act of
charity. (or) Never stop
someone who desires to help
people in need.

5. உடையது விளம்பேல்.

Do not boast about your
possessions and achievements.
(or) Do not sing your own
praises.

6. ஊக்கமது கைவிடேல்.

Never let go your motivation
or enthusiasm during your
efforts.

7. எண்ணெழுத் திகழேல்.

Learn Mathematics and Grammar without contempt (ridicule or dislike).

8. ஏற்ப திகழ்ச்சி.

Accepting or seeking things (begging) from others brings disgrace.

Note: This verse points at people who always make a living by begging from others out of laziness to do any work.

9. ஐய மிட்டுண.

Feed people in need before you eat.

10. ஒப்புர வொழுகு.

Live in harmony with the world. (or) Perform your actions (righteously) in accordance with the world.

11. ஓதுவ தொழியேல்.

Do not stop reading. (or) Seek knowledge continuously.

12. ஒளவியம் பேசேல்.

Do not speak with jealousy. (or) Do not envy others.

13. அஃகஞ் சுருக்கேல்.

Do not reduce the quantity (while selling grains or produce) to make more money. (or) Avoid act of greediness while conducting business.

14. கண்டொான்று சொல்லேல்.

Do not say things that you did not see. (or) Do not be a false witness.

15. நுப்போல் வளை.

Embrace your community and offer your service to others

even if others do not return
your service.

16. சனி நீராடு.

On Saturdays apply oil to your
body and head before taking
bath.

Note: In Indian tradition, oil (sesame
oil) bath at least once a week is
considered good for overall health.

17. இயம்பட வுரை.

Speak pleasantly and bring
happiness to others.

18. இடம்பட வீடெடேல்.

Do not build houses (with surplus unused space) bigger than that for the family size.

19. இணக்கமறிந் திணங்கு.

Understand the moral character of a person before developing friendship.

20. தந்தைதாய்ப் பேண.

Take care of your father and mother (in their old age).

21. நன்றி மறவேல்.

Never forget the help
extended by others to you. (or)
Be grateful to those who
helped you.

22. பருவத்தே பயிர்செய்.

Sow at the right season for
good yield. (or) Act at the
right time to get great results.

23. மண்பறித் துண்ணேல்.

Do not make a living by
exploiting land or other
possessions of others.

24. இயல்பலா தனசெயேல்.

Do not perform any action that does not come to you naturally. (or)

Do not perform any action that involves bad conduct (Good conduct should be your true nature).

25. அரவ மாட்டேல்.

Do not hold poisonous snakes in hand and play.

Note: This verse is mainly to advise young children to be careful and not to be excessively adventurous when they play outdoors especially in rural areas.

26. இலவம்பஞ்சிற் றுயில்.

Sleep on mattress that is made of silk cotton.

Note: This verse is to advise everyone especially children to sleep on mattress made of silk cotton so that they do not develop heat related illness and back(spinal) problems.

27. வஞ்சகம் பேசேல்.

Do not speak deceptive or unfaithful words.

28. அழகலா தனசெயேல்.

Do not perform bad or
shameful actions.

29. இளமையிற் கல்.

Learn when you are young.
(or) Start learning at an early
age.

30. அறனை மறவேல்.

Never fail or forget to
perform righteous actions.

31. அனந்த லாடேல்.

Do not sleep excessively.

32. கடிவது மற.

Do not speak in a rude or
harsh manner to others.

33. காப்பது விரதம்.

To protect other beings
(plants, animals, human) is
everyone's duty. (or) Everyone
should take a vow to protect
other beings.

34. கிழமைப் படவாழ்.

Live to help others physically
and monetarily.

35. கீழ்மை யகற்று.

Get rid of bad things (bad character, bad actions and bad thoughts).

36. குணமது கைவிடேல்.

Do not get rid of good character or good behaviors.

37. கூடிப் பிரியேல்.

Do not get disassociated from a good friend.

38. கெடுப்ப தொழி.

Never intend to do bad things
for others.

39. கேள்வி முயல்.

Make efforts to listen to
teachings from learned people.

40. கைவினை கரவேல்.

Demonstrate (learn or
practice) handicraft skills.

Note: This is suggested perhaps to
promote creativity and self
employment.

41. கொள்ளை
விரும்பேல்.

Do not desire to steal from others.

42. கோதாட் டொழி.

Do not indulge in any sport that requires wrongdoing.

43. கௌவை அகற்று.

Remove grief that is not real. (or) Do not grieve for trivial things.

44. சக்கர நெறி நில்.

Follow the rules laid out by the king (government).

45. சான்றோ ரினத்திரு.

Remain in the company of learned people.

46. சித்திரம் பேசேல்.

Do not speak false words.

47. சீர்மை மறவேல்.

Do not forget the quality (personality trait) that brings glory.

48. சுளிக்கச் சொல்லேல்.

Do not speak to others in a manner that creates anger and hatred.

49. சூது விரும்பேல்.

Do not desire to gamble.

50. செய்வன திருந்தச்செய்.

Anything you do, do it right. (or) Carry out an action after assessing the effect of its outcome and do it impeccably.

51. சேரிடமறிந்து சேர்.

Ensure the goodness of
people before seeking their
friendship.

52. சையெனத் திரியேல்.

Do not wander aimlessly in
life causing displeasure to
others (elders).

53. சொற்சோர்வு படேல்.

Do not speak in a manner that
results in a fault or mistake,
even unintentionally.

54. சோம்பித் திரியேல்.

Do not be lazy (without putting effort) in all your actions.

55. தக்கோ னெனத்திரி.

Conduct yourself properly to earn high regards from others (elders).

56. தானமது விரும்பு.

Love to donate to deserving people.

57. திருமாலுக் கடிமைசெய்.

Serve God. (or) Be loyal to
God

Note: This advises one to develop faith
in God. Here the referred God is Lord
Vishnu in Hindu religion.

58. தீவினை யகற்று.

Avoid doing bad (sinful or
evil) things.

59. துன்பத்திற்
கிடங்கொடேல்.

Do not grieve. (or) Do not
give up your effort because of
the physical pain or mental
strain that arises during your

effort. (or) Avoid unnecessary inconvenience.

60. தூக்கி வினைசெய்.

Start a work with an action plan in mind and complete it.

61. தெய்வ மிகழேல்.

Do not speak ill of God.

62. தேசத்தோ டொத்துவாழ்.

Live in harmony with the citizens of your nation.

63. தையல்சொல் கேளேல்.

Do not listen to the words of people who speak craftily (marked by deviousness or deception).

64. தொன்மை மறவேல்.

Do not forget the old (longstanding) friendship. (or) Do not forget your valuable ancient legacies.

65. தோற்பன தொடரேல்.

Do not continue to indulge in activities that bring failure.

66. நன்மை கடைப்பிடி.

Carry out deeds that bring
good results. (or) Cultivate
good thinking and perform
good actions.

67. நாடொப் பனசெய்.

Perform actions (righteous)
that are accepted by everyone
in the society/country.

68. நிலையிற் பிரியேல்.

Do not slide from the good
position (virtue) you are in.
(or) Do not compromise your
virtues.

69. நீர்விளை யாடேல்.

Do not swim or play in deep waters.

70. நுண்மை நுகரேல்.

Do not eat food that will cause illness. (or) Do not eat spoiled food.

71. நூல்பல கல்.

Read several books that will bring useful knowledge.

72. நெற்பயிர் விளை.

Cultivate grains on your own effort. (or) Practice agriculture.

73. நேர்பட வொழுகு.

Live with good character and integrity.

74. நைவினை நணுகேல்.

Do not perform any evil action that gives sorrow to others.

75. நொய்ய வுரையேல்.

Do not speak words that have no value. (or) Do not speak non sense.

76. நோய்க்கிடங் கொடேல்.

Never allow diseases to affect you. (or) Avoid any illness, by eating well, sleeping well, thinking good and doing good.

77. பழிப்பன பகரேல்.

Do not speak any words (insulting, bad meaning) that bring disgrace to you from people of good virtue.

78. பாம்பொடு பழகேல்.

Do not develop friendship
with evil (dishonest, immoral)
people (bad company is
compared with poisonous
snakes).

79. பிழைபடச்
சொல்லேல்.

Do not utter words that lead
to error or inappropriateness.

80. பீடு பெறநில்.

Follow the moral path that
brings you glory.

81. புகழ்ந்தாரைப் போற்றிவாழ்.

Protect the people who appreciated your achievements or supported you in your accomplishments.

82. பூமி திருத்தியுண்.

Plough arable land and cultivate crops to make your living. (or) Make agriculture as your occupation.

83. பெரியாரைத் துணைக்கொள்.

Seek the company of
experienced and learned
people.

84. பேதைமை யகற்று.

Strive to eradicate ignorance.

85. பையலோ டிணங்கேல்.

Do not associate with playful
irresponsible kids.

86. பொருடனைப் போற்றிவாழ்.

Save your money (wealth) and avoid spending unnecessarily.

87. போர்த்தொழில் புரியேல்.

Do not get involved in a profession that involves war or fight. (or)

Do not make it a habit to get into quarrel or confrontation with others.

88. மனந்தடு மாறேல்.

Do not let your mind become unstable or upset under any circumstances.

89. மாற்றானுக் கிடங்கொடேல்.

Do not let your enemy take advantage and win over you.

90. மிகைபடச் சொல்லேல்.

Do not use fancy words to convey simple meanings. (or) Do not exaggerate things.

91. மீதூண் விரும்பேல்.

Do not indulge in excessive eating.

92. முனைமுகத்து நில்லேல்.

Do not be present in war zone.

93. மூர்க்கரோ டிணங்கேல்.

Avoid the company of people with foolish or irrational thoughts.

94. மெல்லினல்லாள் தோள்சேர்.

Note: Since this book is targeted for younger children also, this quote is

irrelevant to them and hence
meaning is not provided.

95. மேன்மக்கள் சொற்கேள்.

Listen and act according to the
words of wise people.

96. மைவிழியார் மனையகல்.

Note: Since this book is targeted for
younger children also, this quote is
irrelevant to them and hence
meaning is not provided.

97. மொழிவ தறமொழி.

Make your statement with clarity and without any scope for doubt. (or) Speak with certainty and confidence.

98. மோகத்தை முனி.

Curb your desire for non-permanent things. (or) Do not desire and waste your time by going behind things that does not last for a long time.

99. வல்லமை பேசேல்.

Do not boast about your aptitude and ability.

100. வாதுமுற் கூறேல்.

Do not confront and argue
with elders or learned people.

101. வித்தை விரும்பு.

Love to acquire skill sets. (or)
Love to be educated.

102. வீடு பெறநில்.

Follow the path of
righteousness to obtain
liberation or salvation.

103. உத்தம னாயிரு.

Strive to be a person with good virtues.

104. ஊருடன் கூடிவாழ்.

Live united with your community during all times (both good and bad).

105. வெட்டெனப் பேசேல்.

Do not use harsh words that can cause pain (mental or emotional) equivalent to that of a pain from a sharp knife cut.

106. வேண்டி
வினைசெயேல்.

Do not commit evil or wrong
actions deliberately.

107. வைகறைத்
துயிலெழு.

Wake up every day before
sunrise.

Note: Getting up before sunrise results
in clear thinking in mind and it ensures
good health.

108. ஒன்னாரைத்
தேறேல்.

Do not trust your enemies.

109. ஓரஞ் சொல்லேல்.

Do not take sides; try to be impartial (unbiased) in all your interactions and conversations.

Tamil Alphabets

Vowels (12)

அ ஆ இ ஈ

உ ஊ எ ஏ

ஐ ஒ ஓ ஔ

Glotaliser (1)

ஃ

Consonants (18)

க ங ச

ஞ ட ண

த ந ப

ம ய ர

ல வ ழ

ள ற ன

Statue of Auvaiyaar in Marina Beach,
Chennai, Tamil Nadu, India.